Collecting

An Unauthorized Handbook and Price Guide

Jan Lindenberger

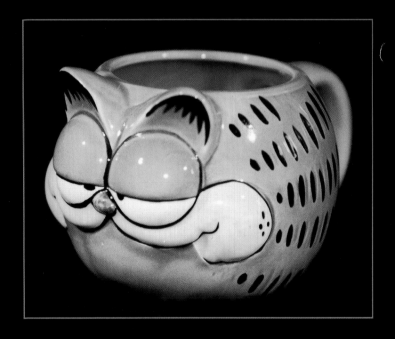

4880 Lower Valley Road, Atglen, PA 19310 USA

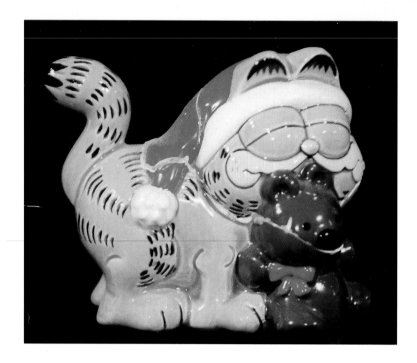

Designed by "Sue"
Typeset in DomBold BT/Souvenir Lt Bt

ISBN: 0-7643-0948-x
Printed in China
1 2 3 4

Published by Schiffer Publishing Ltd.
4880 Lower Valley Road
Atglen, PA 19310
Phone: (610) 593-1777; Fax: (610) 593-2002
e-mail: schifferbk@aol.com
Please visit our website catalog at
www.schifferbooks.com
or write for a free printed catalog.
This book may be purchased from the publisher.
Please include $3.95 for shipping.

In Europe, Schiffer books are distributed by
Bushwood Books
6 Marksbury Avenue
Kew Gardens
Surrey TW9 4JF England
Phone: 44 (0)208 392-8585; Fax: 44 (0)208 392-9876
e-mail: bushwd@aol.com

Please try your bookstore first.

We are interested in hearing from authors with book ideas on related subjects.

Contents

Acknowledgments

I wish to thank my son Tom Knight and his wife Cindy, from Colorado Springs, Colorado, for unpacking all their Garfield collectibles for me to photograph. When their three children saw all the fun things they had, they wanted Mommy and Daddy to leave them out....Maybe we have three new collectors now! Thanks to Susan Williams for allowing me to photograph her vast collection of Garfield memorabilia. Susan is from Colorado Springs, Colorado, and is an Interior Decorator. Also, thanks to Joey, Debbie, Shannon, Paula, Brandi, and Anita (from Walmart photo lab) for taking the time to make sure the photos were just right!

Miranda, Preston and Kayla Knight (grandchildren of the author) with stuffed Garfield's from their collection.

Introduction

Garfield is an orange, lazy, sleepy, lasagna eating cat. He was born on June 19, 1978 and created by Jim Davis, cartoonist and animator. Jim Davis was born in July of 1945, on a farm, in Marion, Indiana. His father, Jim Davis Sr., his mother, Betty, and his brother Dave, raised black Angus cows on their farm along with several cats. As a child, Jim Jr. was ill with athsma and had to stay indoors much of the time. In his recuperating time he amused himself by drawing and, discovered that he was good at it. He kept drawing throughout his youth and ended up going to Ball State University where he met and married his wife Carolyn. After Jim graduated he worked for four years at an advertising agency. Then, in 1969, he joined "Tumbleweed" creator, Tom Ryan, as his cartoon assistant and created a character named "Gnorm Gnat." This comic strip was successful and ran in the Indiana Newspaper for five years. After the cartoon ended, Jim drew a large foot that seemed to come out of the sky, crushing the Gnorm, and officially ended the cartoon.

Davis continuously noticed that there were several comic strips about dogs but nothing about cats. Realizing this and the fact that there were many cat lovers in the world, (he was one as he was raised with 25 cats on the farm), he created Garfield. Davis states (according to the www.Garfield.com website), "I keep rhyming gags, plays on words or colloquialisms out of the strip, in an effort to make Garfield apply virtually to any society where he may appear, dealing with only sleeping and eating." This is only part of Garfield's, the lasagna loving cat, success. In 1981, Jim Davis formed his company, "Paws Inc.," to oversee all of the Garfield products on the market. Jim personally makes sure each item meets his approval and maintains the finest quality before it is marketed. Today, Garfield appears on thousands of products sold around the world. In 1981 and 1986 the National Cartoonist Society named Jim Davis the best humor comic strip. He also received the Reuben Award, in 1990, from N C S, for most outstanding comic strip of the year.

Garfield has just celebrated his 20th birthday, and I believe he celebrated it by being hungry and by having a very large cake. He has not changed his attitude in the past 20 years but, Garfield does look friendlier now. I hope you enjoy this information and price guide on Garfield collectibles. Please use it on your hunt for Garfield collectibles. Prices may vary according to state location, condition and availability. Also, shop prices may vary from flea market price to garage sale price. Some of the items in this "Garfield Collectibles Information and Price Guide" are still available and very collectible!

Chapter One: Kitchen

Aluminum mug with clear plastic bottom. 4 3/4", $30-40.

Ceramic mug. Enesco. $5-10.

Front and back of ceramic mug. "Vote
Garfield, Vote Democratic." Enesco. $5-10.

Ceramic cup. "World's Greatest Baby Sitter." Enesco. $5-10.

Ceramic mug. Enesco. "Last Call." 4.5", $25-35.

Ceramic mug. Enesco. "Downhill all the way." 4.5", $25-35. (Not shown: Garfield getting into fishbowl, "Call it an ethnic weakness," and Garfield hanging on outside of cup "I resent that.", $25-35 each).

Ceramic mug. Enesco. "Ta-Dah! Class of '86." 4.5", $25-35.

Ceramic smiling Garfield mug. Paws. 3", $15-25.

Ceramic Garfield showing teeth mug. 3", $15-25.

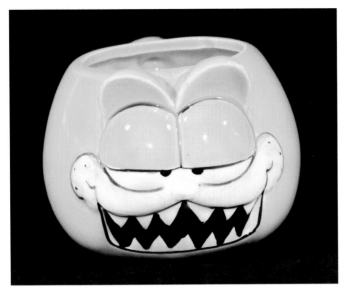

Ceramic Garfield showing teeth mug. 3", $15-25.

Glass mugs from McDonalds. Front and back view. $10-15 each.

Juice glasses (4 oz.) and quart pitcher. $25-35 for set of 4 glasses and pitcher.

Front and back of plastic cups from Pizza Hut. Pizza Hut promo. Early 1990s. $5-7 each.

Plastic cups with lids and straws. Front and back view. 10 oz. $5-7 each.

Plastic Garfield bowl. Front and back view. Deka Plastics, NJ 5.5", $20-25.

Popcorn tin. Front and back view. 12", $20-30.

Metal Garfield container. "Light-
hearted." Cheinco. 3/4", $10-15.

Aluminum cake pan with plastic face and instructions. Wilton Cake Co. $30-40.

Garfield cookie tin. Giftco. Front and back view. 6.5", $10-15.

Garfield tin. "Sleep conserves energy." 4", $8-12.

Plastic coasters. Conimar. 4", $6-10.

Plastic paper cup dispenser. 7", $15-20.

Vinyl place-mat. "Feed Me." Free with case of 13oz. Alpo
cat food purchase. 1980s. 11" x 16", $10-12.

Franco American Garfield pasta.
(Also came with beef in pizza sauce
and pizza O's in pizza sauce.)
$8-10 each.

Chocolate Garfield valentine. Allen Co. Bortz Chocolate. 6.5", $6-10.

Picture of Garfield and his eating tips. United Features. 9.5" x 14", $20-25.

20

Ceramic figurine of Santa Garfield and his bear, Pooky. Enesco. 4", $25-35.

Below: Ceramic figurine of walking Santa Garfield and his teddy bear, Pooky. Enesco. 3.5", $25-35.

Ceramic figurine of Garfield in Christmas stocking. Enesco. 3", $25-35.

Ceramic figurine of Garfield in tuxedo. Enesco. 5", $25-35.

Ceramic figurine of Arlene (Garfield's girlfriend). Enesco. 4", $40-50.

22

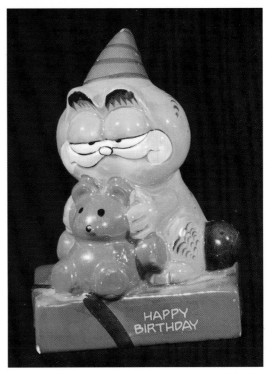

Ceramic figurine of Garfield playing baseball. "Baseball players pop-up in the strangest places." Enesco. 4.5", $25-35.

Ceramic figurine of Garfield with his teddy bear, Pooky. "Happy Birthday." Enesco. 4.5", $25-35.

Ceramic figurine of Garfield skiing. "Schuss Cat." Enesco. 4", $25-35.

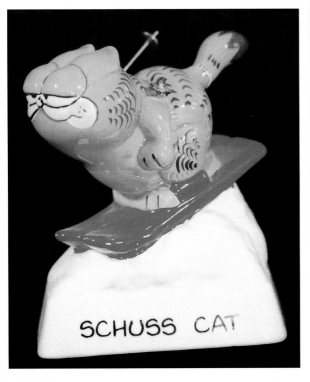

Ceramic figurine of Garfield with valentine. "I'm All Yours." Enesco. 3", $25-35.

23

Rubber mini figure of
Garfield with his arms
folded. 2", $6-10.

Ceramic Garfield holding birthday cake. "Blow Out The
Candle And Let's Eat." Enesco. 3 3/4", $25-35.

Rubber figure of Garfield
holding his bear, Pooky. 2.5",
$5-8.

Rubber bendable and poseable Garfield. "Kiss me you
fool." Dakin, Inc. 5", $15-20. (Not shown: "Am I cool or
what?" "Take me I'm yours.", $15-20 each).

Plastic trophy of Garfield looking in the mirror. "Where have you been all my life?" Aviva. 4.5", $10-15.

Plastic trophy of Garfield getting his back scratched. "Some People Rub Me The Wrong Way." Aviva. 5", $10-15.

Plastic Garfield trophy. Push bottom of figure and his mouth opens to show his teeth. "Pooky Is A One Cat Teddy Bear." 3.5", $10-15.

Plastic Garfield trophy with Pooky. "I'm Only Human." Push bottom of figure and he opens and closes his eyes. 3.5", $10-15. (Others not shown: "When it comes to eating, I'm a genius," and "Take me home and feed me.", $10-15).

Plastic Garfield trophy's. Left is Garfield: "I Never Met A Lasagna I Didn't Like." Push bottom and his mouth opens. Right: "I'm Not Known For My Compassion." Push bottom and he opens his eyes. 3.5", $10-15 each.

Plastic Garfield trophy's. Left Garfield: "Big Fat Hairy Deal." Push bottom and his head moves back and forth. Right Garfield: "Never Trust A Smiling Cat." Push bottom and his mouth opens. 3.5", $10-15 each.

Plastic Garfield trophy. "I hate cute." Push bottom and his eyes open and close. 3.5", $10-15.

Rubber skier figure. 2", $10-15.

Rubber Garfield, with Pooky, in a plastic car. 2.5", $10-15.

Rubber Garfield and Odie on plastic scooter. McDonalds give away. 3", $10-15.

Plastic Garfield on skateboard. McDonalds give away. 3", $10-15.

Plastic Garfield sitting on plastic skateboard. McDonalds give away. 3",
$10-15.

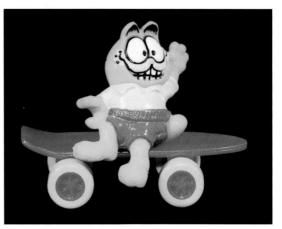

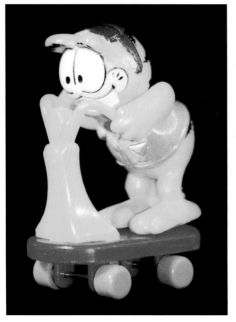

Plastic Garfield on scooter. McDonalds
give away. 3", $10-15.

Plastic Garfield on scooter.
McDonalds give away.
3", $10-15.

Plastic Garfield on scooter.
McDonalds give away. 3",
$10-15.

29

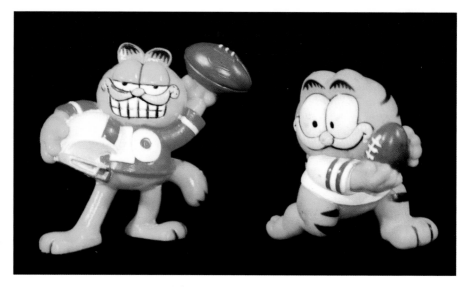

Plastic Garfield figures. 2.5", $5-10 each. (Also available but not shown: Jogger, basketball player, baseball player, batter, Garfield with beach ball, Odie sitting, Odie laying, and Garfield in fur coat. $5-10 each).

Plastic Garfield playing soccer. 2.5", $5-10.

Plastic sports' Garfield's. 2"-2.5", $5-10 each.

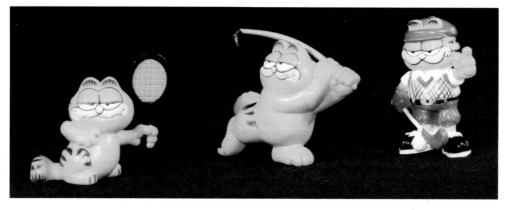

Rubber Garfield figures. 3/4",
$5-10 each.

Rubber Santa Garfield figure. 2", $8-12.

Rubber figure of Garfield in a
package. Paws, Inc. 3 3/4", $6-10.

Rubber Garfield in St. Patrick's bag.
"Kiss me, get lucky!" 2.5", $10-15.

Garfield playing football, candle. Enesco.
2 1/4", $8-12.

Garfield "Humble" candle. Enesco. 3" x 6", $8-12.

Plastic alarm clock. Sunbeam. 14", $60-75.

Giant plastic alarm clock.
Sunbeam. 18", $85-125.

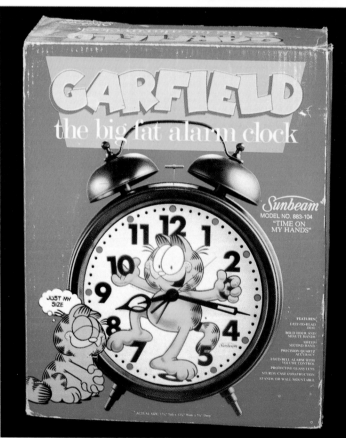

Giant plastic alarm clock
with box. Sunbeam.
18", $100-150.

PERSONALIZED WALL CLOCK

Keep time with America's favorite feline. Cool clock is 10¼" wide, and features second hand and clear acrylic face. Outer rim is available in four fun colors: red, black, white, and gold-tone. Specify up to 2 lines, limit 12 letters and spaces maximum per line. AA battery (not included).

Personalized Wall Clock #501525 $39.95

18

Personalized wall clock. (Picture from Garfield catalogue, 1997) 10 1/4", $50-75.

Plastic Garfield clock. Battery operated. Tail and eyes move back and forth. Sunbeam. 16", $70-100.

Metal Garfield alarm clock. Sunbeam. 4" x 6", $50-75.

35

Electric, plastic Garfield face
clock. The time is displayed
in his teeth. Squeeze his ear
to set alarm. Squeeze his
nose and it turns off.
Sunbeam. 7", $50-75.

Plastic, 2 gallon, electric
Garfield fish tank. 18",
$125-175.

Plastic Garfield telephone. Pick up the receiver and he opens his eyes. Buttons are in the receiver. Kash N Gold Ltd. $75-100. (Also available but not shown: another version of sleeping Garfield phone. Coloring different. $125-150. Garfield with movable head tilted to the side with white claws. Tyco Indus. $150-175. Garfield holding phone in his paws. Push button and he says Yoo- Hoo, etc. Tyco Indus. $125-175).

Plush Garfield wearing plush Garfield slippers. Dakin. 12", $50-75.

Plush "Cattygram, Love from Lightning Lips" Garfield. Dakin. 9.5", $40-60.

Plush Garfield wearing fur coat and Garfield pin. Dakin. 10", $50-75.

Plush Garfield on surfboard. Dakin. 9", $35-45.

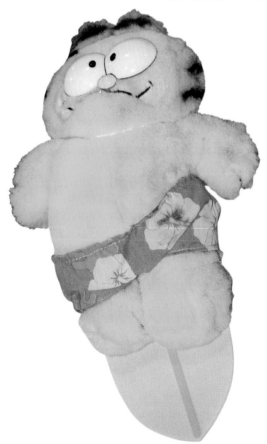

Plush Garfield on skateboard wearing sweat suit. "Life in the fast lane." Dakin. 8", $35-45.

Plush Garfield in swimsuit, wearing Odie as a life saver. Dakin. 9", $40-50.

Plush Garfield wearing a toothless smile with plush tooth. Dakin. 9", $50-75.

Plush Garfield as a
baseball player. Dakin.
9", $35-45.

Plush Garfield on sled.
Dakin. 8", $35-45.

41

Plush Garfield the Chef. Dakin. 10",
$40-50.

Plush Garfield as a cook with
his bowl of food and spoon.
Dakin. 9". $45-55.

Plush Garfield sitting with his scarf and ear muffs. 12", $45-55.

Plush Garfield holding a plastic heart. 12", $35-45.

Plush Santa Garfield with beard and hat. Dakin. 8", $25-35.

Plush Garfield wearing sweatshirt. "1 USA."
Dakin. 8", $35-45.

Plush Garfield wearing collegiate shirt.
Dakin. 7", $35-45.

Plush Easter Garfield holding basket.
Dakin. 12", $45-50.

Plush Garfield with his leather football. Dakin. 9", $35-45.

Plush Garfield's holding satin hearts. Dakin. 9", $35-45.

Plush Garfield in his leather, fleece- lined, coat and hat with plastic goggles. Dakin. 8", $50-60.

Plush, bean bag, Garfield in baseball outfit. Dakin. 8", $35-45.

Plush graduate Garfield wearing a plastic hat. Dakin. 5", $30-40.

Plush baseball Garfield sitting with his dangling feet. He's wearing a blue and white stripped hat and shirt. Dakin. 9", $35-45.

Plush "Love Struck!" Garfield with felt shirt and hat. Dakin. 8", $30-40.

Plush sitting Garfield "I'm not Fat I'm under tall!" Dakin. 9", $35-45.

Plush devil Garfield wearing a red hat and cape. Dakin. 6", $30-40.

Plush devil Garfield with plastic tag. 9", $35-45.

Plush Garfield in pajamas and bunny slippers with Pooky. Dakin. 10", $40-50.

Plush bean bag Garfield sitting.
Dakin. 5.5", $20-30.

Plush Garfield dressed as a fleece lamb.
Dakin. 9", $50-60.

Plush Garfield, with light stripes, sitting.
Dakin. 6", $20-30.

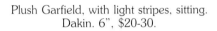

Plush Garfield, with darker stripes, sitting.
Dakin. 6", $30-40.

Plush Garfield, with darker stripes, sitting. Dakin. 9", $35-45.

Plush Garfield sitting with out-stretched paws and half open eyes. Dakin. 6", $30-40.

Plush, fat cat, sitting Garfield. Dakin. 15", $40-45.

Plush Garfield sitting with wide open eyes. Front and
back view. Came with pin. Dakin. 6", $30-40.

Plush Garfield sitting with dangling feet.
Dakin. 9", $30-40.

Plush Santa Garfield. Window
sticker. Dakin. 9", $30-40.

Plush walking Garfield. Dakin.
10", $25-35.

Plush Garfield window stickers. Front and back view. Came with pins.
Dakin. 7", $30-40 each.

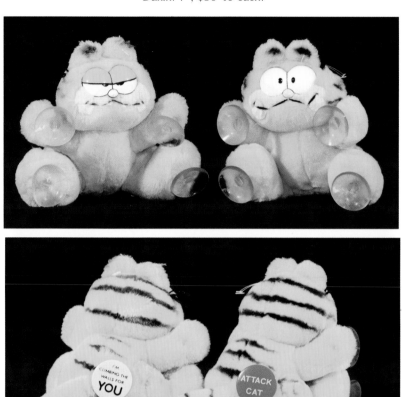

Below and right:
Plush Garfield with wide teeth showing.
Window sticker. Dakin. 7", $30-40.

Plush Garfield window sticker wearing red heart shorts. Front and back view. Came with button. Dakin. 6", $30-40.

Felt, talking Garfield with plastic moving eyes. Pull string in back and he talks as he moves his eyes. Mattel. 9", $50-75.

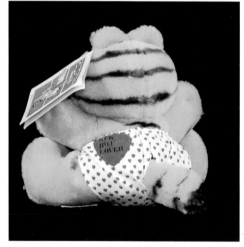

Felt, talking Garfield with plastic moving eyes. Pull string and he moves his eyes as he talks. Mattel. 9", $50-75.

Felt, talking Garfield with plastic moving eyes. Pull string and he moves his eyes as he talks. Mattel. 10", $50-75.

Sitting Garfield made of synthetic fabric. Cloth eyes by Fun Farm. 7", $20-30.

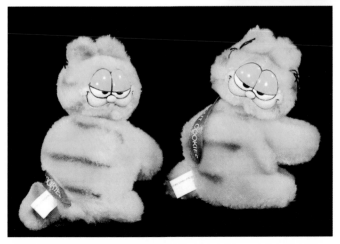

Plush clip-on Garfield's. Dakin. 3.5", $10-15.

Plush clip-on Santa Garfield. 6", $10-15.

Plush Garfield hand puppet. Note the darker color inside his ears. Dakin. 10". $20-30.

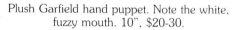

Plush Garfield hand puppet. Note the white, fuzzy mouth. 10", $20-30.

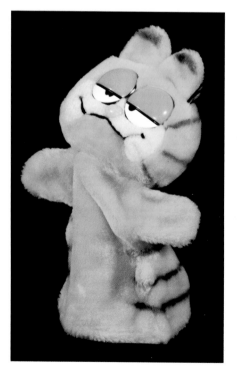

Plush Garfield hand puppet. Note the lighter color inside his ears. Dakin. 11". $20-30.

Plush Garfield window scraper. 11", $20-30.

Plush Arlene and Odie. 7" Arlene. 7" & 8" Odie. Dakin. $20-30 each.

Plush Odie sitting and wearing a hat that says "Dummy." Dakin. 7", $30-40.

Plush Nermal missing his pacifier. Dakin. 9", $30-40.

Synthetic stuffed Garfield pillow. Plush Creations. 26", $40-50.

Cloisonne Garfield pins. Kats Meow. $8-10 each.

Metal pin, back button. "Start each day with a
smile and get over with." 6", $10-15.

Plastic play watch
with Odie on the
face. Duram, Indus.
$10-15.

Right and below: Plastic play watch. Armitron. Late 1990s. $20-25.

Plastic watch with Garfield on face. Armitron. $30-40.

Above and left: Metal Armitron watch and case. Early 1990s. $40-50.

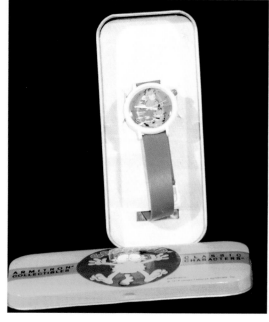

Right: Metal and leather watch and case. Armitron. $40-50.

Right:
Plastic Garfield Christmas
ornament. Matrix, Ind.
1980s. 2.5", $30-40.

Plastic Garfield Christmas ornaments. Matrix, Ind. 1980s. 2.5".
$30-40 each.

Plastic mini Garfield ornaments. Paws Gifts Inc. China.
$20-30 set.

Plastic Garfield Christmas ornaments. 20 years of Garfield. Matrix, Ind.
Late 1990s. 2"-3.5", $25-35 each.

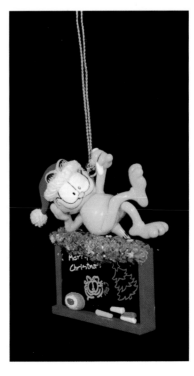

Cardboard display case for Garfield ornaments. Late 1990s. $50-75.

Chapter Seven: **Toys**

Vinyl blow up Garfield with box. Imperial. 42" tall, $50-75 (Shown with Preston Knight, grandson of the author).

Plastic yo-yo from Avon.
2.5", $10-15.

Plastic riding Garfield toy. Early
1980s. $75-100.

Plastic bubble gum machine.
Superior Toy Co. 7" x 7", $35-45.
(Please see collectible section
listings for more "not shown"
bubble gum machines).

Vinyl, inflatable blow up toy.
Given by Pizza Hut. 8", $7-10.

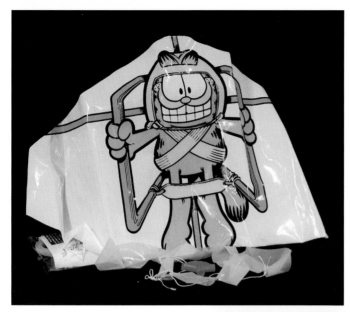

Left and below:
Vinyl kite and rubber
Garfield. Given by
Pizza Hut. China. 17"
x 14", $7-10.

Rubber Garfield with Pooky,
bank. 6", $20-30.

Rubber Garfield sitting in rubber ducky
inner tube. 2.5", $6-10.

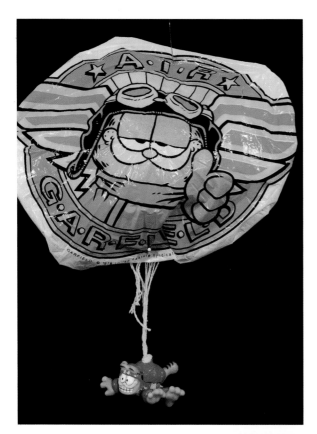

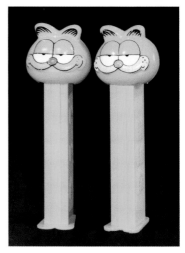

Plastic Garfield Pez candy dispensers. Late 1980s. (Also available but not shown are Arlene, Pilot Garfield with hat and goggles, Odie, Sleepy Garfield with night cap, Chef Garfield with bakers hat, Garfield with visor, Nermal, Smiling Garfield) $7-10 each.

Vinyl parachute and rubber Garfield. "Air Garfield." Given by Pizza Hut. 10" x 12", $7-10.

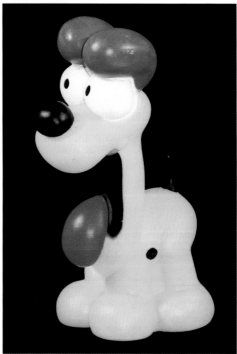

Rubber Odie bank. Kats Meow. 8", $20-30.

Wooden paddle and ball game.
Unique Indus. 10", $10-15.

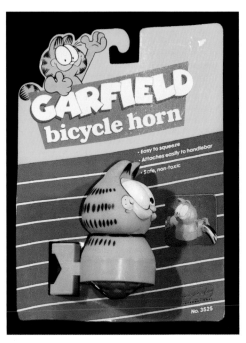

Rubber bike horn. A/C International. $6-12.

Plastic Garfield bike reflector. NCM
Corp. 3", $7-10.

Plastic Frisbee given by Reading Club. 7", $4-6.

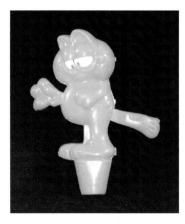

Plastic Garfield pencil topper and toy. Pull Garfield's tail and he opens his eyes. (Also available but not shown is pink Odie, pull tail and his tongue goes up and down) $7-10 each.

Rubber baby Garfield squeeze toy. Garfield playing with blocks. Remco Baby Inc. 3.5", $10-15.

Plastic toy lock. 3", $2-3.

Rubber Garfield head. Squeeze him and he blows bubbles. 1.5", $5-7.

Rubber baby squeeze toy with plastic rattle on top of cone. Remco Baby Inc. $7-10.

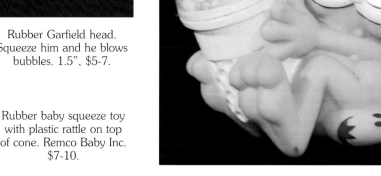

Rubber baby squeeze toy. Garfield in
pajamas and slippers. Remco Baby Inc.
4", $7-10.

Plastic baby rattle.
Garfield's head. Remco
Baby Inc. 3", $6-10.

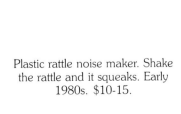

Plastic Garfield rattle. Garfield holding rattle
sitting on top of a safety pin. Remco Baby
Inc. 4.5", $6-10.

Plastic rattle noise maker. Shake
the rattle and it squeaks. Early
1980s. $10-15.

Hard plastic Garfield, standing on his head, baby rattle. (Also available as "It's a Girl"). Remco Baby Inc. 5", $5-10.

Plastic bucket from Subway Sandwich Shops. (Other bucket has Garfield sitting in sports car). Berry Plastics. 5" x 7", $10-15.

Plastic baby rattle with Garfield in center of circle. Remco Baby Inc. 4.5", $5-10.

Poster puzzle. Over 500 pieces. 15" x 21", $8-12.

Cardboard puzzle. Golden. 11" x 14", $8-12.

Wooden puzzle from Playskool.
7 pieces. $8-12.

Cardboard puzzle from Golden. 200
pieces. $8-12.

Cardboard puzzle from Golden. 100 pieces.
11.5" x 15", $8-12.

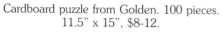

Cardboard puzzle from Golden. 100
pieces. 11.5" x 15", $8-12.

Cardboard puzzle from Golden. 11.5" x 15", $8-12.

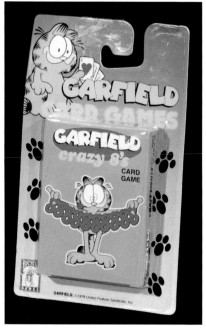

Garfield, Crazy Eight's, card game. US Playing Card Co. $5-8.

Cardboard puzzle from American Publishing. 18" x 24", $10-15.

Garfield board game from Parker Bros. 1981. $20-30.

Plastic, Kitty Letters, game from Parker Bros. Let sticks drop and try to make a word without moving other sticks. $15-20.

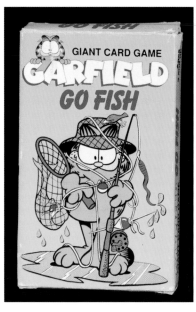

Garfield, Go Fish, card game. US Playing Card Co. $5-8.

Garfield, Old Maid, card game. US Playing Card Co. $5-8 each.

Garfield, Magic Cards #1, card game. US Playing Card Co. $5-8.

Chapter Nine: School Time

Three ring "Whiz Kitty" notebook. $5-8.

Right and top right:
Front and back of three ring
notebook from Mead Co. $5-10.

Paper school folder from Pizza Hut.
Front and back. Early 1990s. $7-10.

Plastic school scissors in
package. Empire Berol,
China. $6-10.

Rubber pencil (pen) holder. Garfield holding a
package. Bully W. Germany. $10-15.

Rubber pencil topper. Arlene in airplane. 2", $4-6.

School tablet from Mead Co. 6" x 8", $4-6.

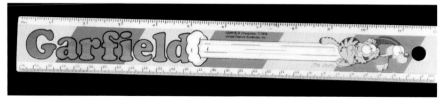

Plastic school ruler. $5-8.

Rubber pencil topper. Garfield with Pooky. Hong Kong. 1.5", $4-6.

Vinyl pencil pouch. Garfield pulling towel from Odie. $8-12.

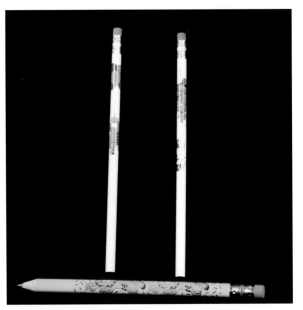

Rubber pencil topper. Garfield holding out his arms. 1.5", $4-6.

Garfield pencils. $3-4 each.

Left: Paper bookmarks. $4-5 each.

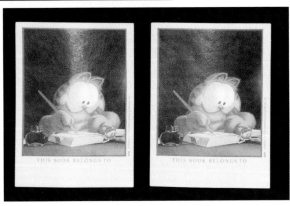

Paper bookmarks. Antioch Pub. Yellow Springs, Ohio. $4-5 each.

Laminated paper bookmark. $4-5.

Magic slate. Golden. $8-12.

Write on and wipe off slate with pen. The Holes-Webway Co. 7", $10-15.

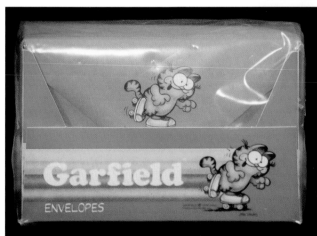

Package of blue enve-
lopes from Mead Co.
$10-15.

Plastic thermos.
Front and back view.
$8-15 each.

Plastic lunch box. Thermos,
USA. $15-20.

Metal lunch box. Front and back view. 5" x 6", $15-20.

Plastic bookmark. 2", $3-4.

Paper lunch bag. Conemar Co.
$2-3 each.

Metal waste paper can. Front and back view. $25-35.

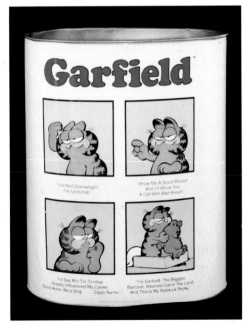

Metal waste paper can. Front and back view. $25-35.

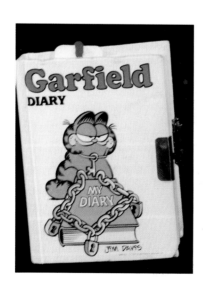

Garfield diary. Holes-Webway.
$15-20.

Garfield diary with key. Late 1980s. $15-20.

Garfield lap table. 16", $15-20.

Chapter Ten: Books

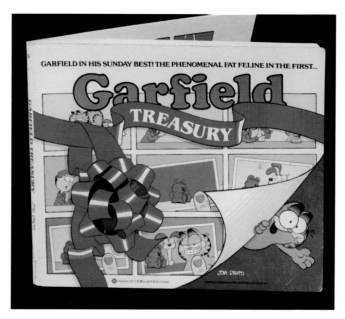

Garfield Treasury. Ballantine. $15-20.

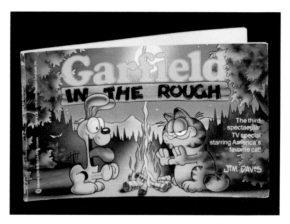

Garfield In The Rough. Ballantine. 1980. $15-20.

Garfield's Picnic Adventure. Golden Books.
Western Pub. Co.
1988. $5-7.

Garfield The Pirate. Random House. 1982.
$5-7.

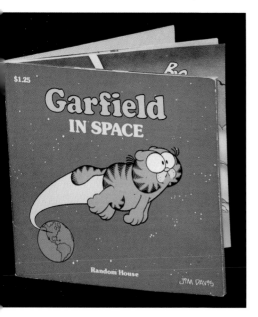

Garfield In Space. Random House. $5-7.

Garfield The Magician. Landoll's. $5-7.

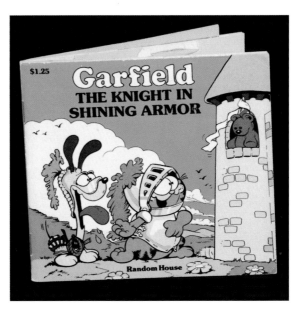

Garfield The Knight In Shining Armor. Random House. $5-7.

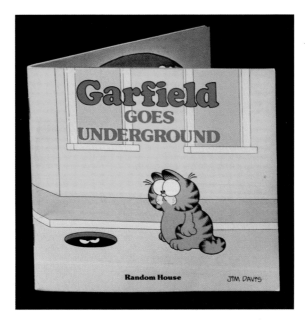

Garfield Goes Underground. Random House. $5-7.

Garfield Goes To A Picnic. Scratch and sniff book.
Random House. 1980s. $7-10.

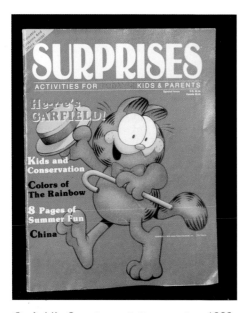

Garfield's *Surprises* activity magazine. 1989.
$8-12.

Garfield's Pet Force. Scholastic Books.
1997. $7-10.

Garfield's Scary Tales, Garfield Discovers America, Garfield's Tales of Mystery. $7-10 each.

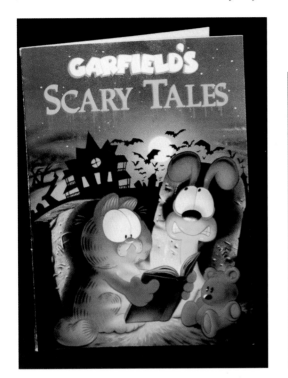

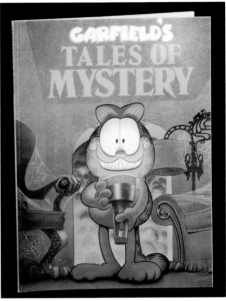

Garfield At Large. Book #1. Ballantine Books. $10-15.

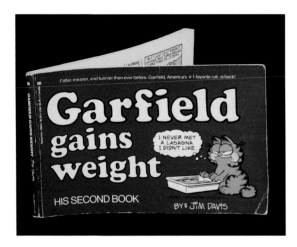

Garfield Gains Weight. Book #2. $10-15.

Garfield Bigger Than Life. Book #3. $10-15.

Garfield Weighs In. Book #4. $10-15.

Garfield Takes The Cake. Book #5. $10-15.

Garfield Eats His Heart Out. Book #6. $10-15.

Garfield Sits Around The House.
Book #7. $10-15.

Garfield Tips The Scales. Book #8. $10-15. (Not shown:
Book #9 Garfield Looses His Feet. Book #10 Garfield
Makes It Big. Book #11 Garfield Rolls On).

Garfield Out To Lunch.
Book #12. $10-15. (Not
shown: Book #13 Garfield
Food For Thought. Book
#14 Garfield Swallows His
Pride. Book #15 Garfield
World Wide. Book #16
Garfield Rounds Out).

Garfield Chews The Fat. Book #17.
$10-15. (Not shown: Book #18
Garfield Goes To Waist. Book #19
Garfield Hangs Out).

Garfield Takes Up Space. Book #20. $10-15.

Garfield Says A Mouthful.
Book #21. $10-15. (Other
Ballantine Books not shown:
Book #22 Garfield By The
Pound. Book #23 Garfield
Keeps His Chin. Book #24
Garfield Takes His Licks. Book
#25 Garfield Hits The Big
Time. Book #26 Garfield Pulls
His Weight. Book #27 Garfield
Dishes It Out. Book #28
Garfield Life In The Fat Lane.
Book #29 Garfield Tons Of
Fun. Book #30 Garfield Bigger
And Better. Book #31 Garfield
Hams It Up. Book #32
Garfield Thinks Big.)
$10-15 each.

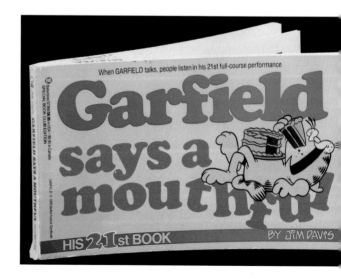

The Fifth Garfield Fat Cat 3-Pack Book. $15-20.

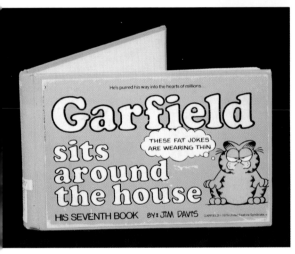

Left:
Hard cover black and white book.
Garfield Sits Around The House.
1983. $18-20.

Garfield's Longest Catnap. Golden. 1989. $5-7.

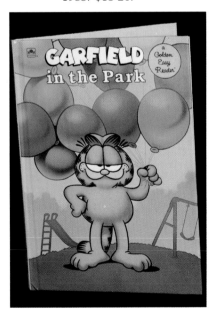

Hard cover story book. *Garfield In The Park.* Golden. 1989. $5-7.

97

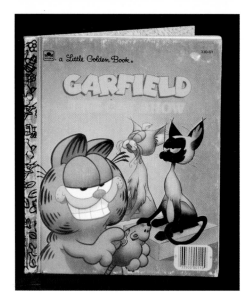

Garfield The Cat Show.
Little Golden Book.
1990. $5-8.

Coloring book. *Merry Christmas Garfield!* Happy House.
1984. $5-7.

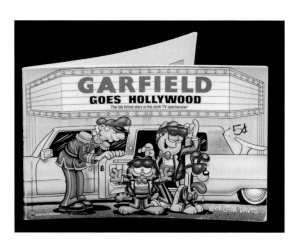

Garfield Goes Hollywood. 1987. $10-15.

The Garfield Trivia Book. $10-15.

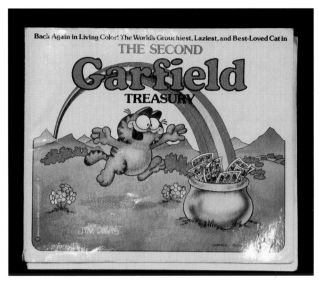

The Second Garfield Treasury. Hard cover. 1983. $15-20.

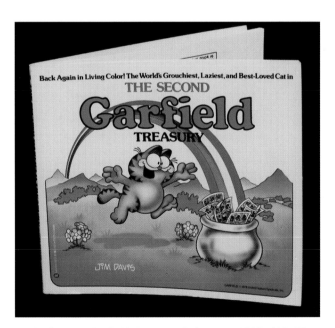

The Second Garfield Treasury. Soft cover. 1983. $10-15.

Garfield book. *I Miss You Most When..* (Shows some of the inside pages). Great graphics. $10-15.

The Fifth Garfield Treasury. Ballantine Books. $10-15.

Garfield Thinking Of You. 30 full- color postcards. 1989.
$10-15.

Garfield's Birthday Surprise. Sticker book. (Inside also). Antioch Pub. 1987. $8-12.

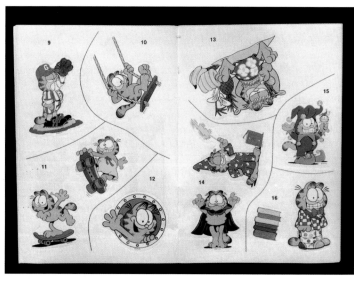

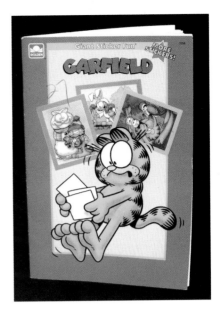

Garfield sticker book. Golden. 1990s.
$5-8.

Garfield Puzzles book. Golden. 1991. $6-9.

Garfield The Sportin' Life. Coloring
and activity book. Landoll's. $5-6.

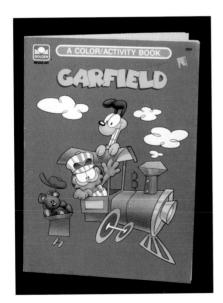

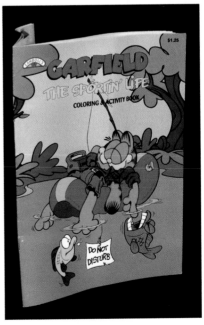

Garfield: A color and activity book.
1991. $5-8.

Garfield Stuff Catalogues. Garfield collectibles that
can be ordered. $5-10 each.

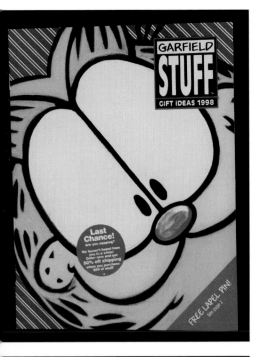

Garfield credit card application. $5-8 pamphlet.

Garfield calendar showing some of the pages. Great graphics. $10-15.

Neptune, the bumbling god of the sea, inadvertently wipes out a small village with a tidal wave of drool.

The goddess Arlena gets stood up by Garcissus, who decides it would be more fun to date himself.

Garfield 1996 calendar
showing some of the pages.
Great graphics. $10-15.

Paper party blow
outs. $3-4 each.

Large plastic shopping bag. 30" x 24", $7-10.

Garfield gift bag. Maryland
Pk'g Corp. $2-3.

Garfield gift bag. Carrousel
Prods. $3-4.

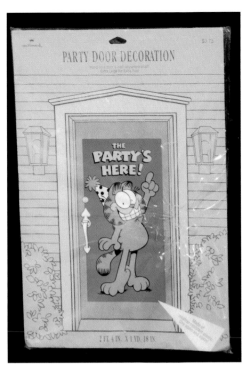

Vinyl party door decoration. Hallmark. $15-20.

Gibson party invitations. $3-5.

Hallmark party invitations. $3-5.

Paper party napkins. Hallmark. $2-3.

Paper party napkins. Gibson. $2-3.

Paper party napkins. Hall-mark. $2-3.

Hallmark wrapping paper. $4-5.

Party table cover made of waffle paper. $10-15.

Cardboard car freshener. 3", $3-4.

Cardboard car freshener. 3", $3-4.

Laminated door knob hanger. Don't disturb sign. "Maid, please make up this room," "invade my place and I'll rearrange your face." (Others not shown are "Genius at work" and "Enter at your own risk.") $5-7.

Cardboard car window cover. $20-25.

Chapter Twelve: Greeting Cards

Buzza greeting card. $3-4.

Gibson greeting card. $3-4.

Buzza greeting card. $3-4.

Gibson greeting card. $3-4.

Hallmark greeting cards. $3-4.

Another Hallmark greeting card. $3-4.

Gibson greeting cards. $3-4 each

Garfield post card. "POW! Lets party." $3-4.

Tile picture/trivet. Enesco. $20-25.

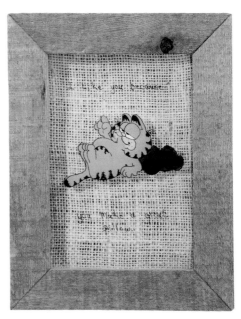

Glass handmade picture. 7" x 9", $7-10.

Tile picture/trivet. Enesco. $20-25.

Resin sun catcher. Makit bakeit. 4", $7-10.

Glass reverse painted picture. 8" x 8", $10-15.

Leaded glass Garfield window hanger. 6" x 9", $20-25.

Garfield banner on rollers. Window shade. $18-22.

Cardboard valentine decoration. 11", $3-4.

Garfield poster. 14" x 21", $8-10.

Garfield poster. Argus.
9" x 13.5", $10-12.

Garfield poster. 14" x 21", $8-10.

Garfield poster.
Argus. 13.5" x 19",
$8-10.

Chapter Fourteen: Wardrobe and Linens

Front and back of cotton tee- shirt.
$6-10.

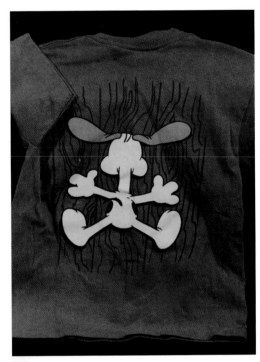

Cotton sweat shirt. "I love girl scout cookies." $7-10.

Cotton hooded sweat shirt. "2 cool 4 words.", $7-10.

Cotton tee- shirt. "Garfield." $7-10.

Plush slippers. (Garfield and Odie) Photo from "Garfield
Stuff" catalogue. $20-25 pair.

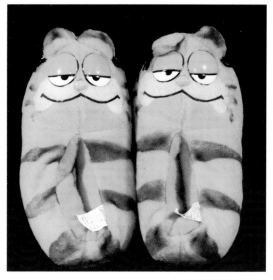

Plush children's' slippers with plastic eyes. $15-20.

Plush adult slippers with plastic eyes. $15-20.

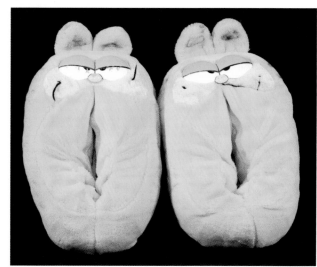

Plush child's slippers with velour eyes. $15-20.

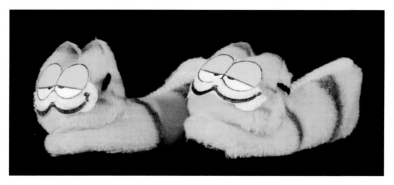

Plush child's slippers
with rubber heads and
leather bottoms.
$15-20.

Cotton Garfield hat with paw prints on top. $15-20.

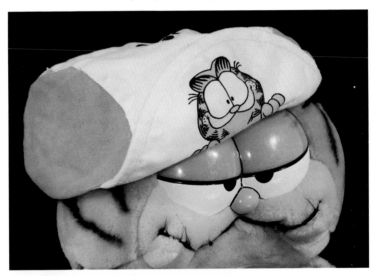

Plastic Garfield bibs. 11" x 12", $5-8 each.

Plastic shoe string holders. $8-12.

Terry- cloth cotton hand towel. $3-4.

Terry- cloth cotton towel. "Tis the season."
$3-4.

Cotton toilet seat cover. 14", $7-10.

Cotton quilted place mat. 13" x 18", $6-10.

Cotton bath mat. Enesco. 1979. $15-20.

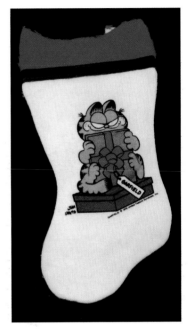

Felt Christmas stocking. 15",
$10-15.

Vinyl child's purse. 6" x 9", $6-8.

Cotton, full- size. sheets. $5-10 each.

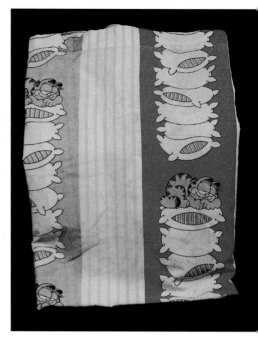

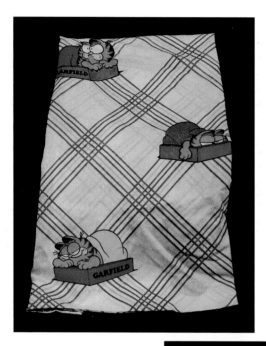

Cotton pillow cases. $4-5 each.

Cotton pillow cases. $4-5 each.

Cotton sheet and pillow case sets. $10-15 set.

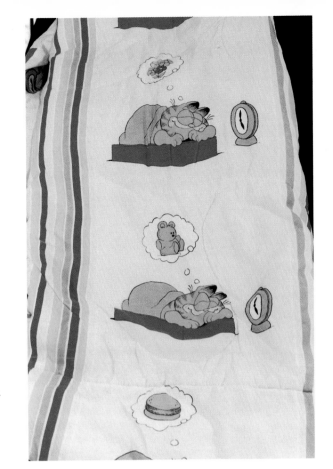

Cotton sleeping bag. $20-30.

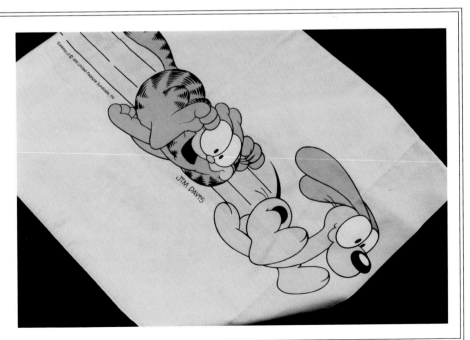

Cotton curtains. $6-10.

Millcraft cross stitch kit. 8 different designs. $8-12.

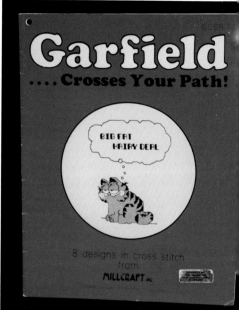

Garfield hook- rug kit.
Millcraft. 12" x 12", $8-12.

Plastic Garfield brush and box. Avon. $20-25.

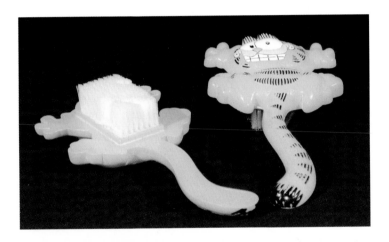

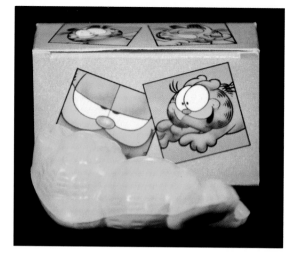

Garfield soap and box. Avon. $8-10.

Rubber Garfield soap dish and soap. Avon. 1991. $20-25.

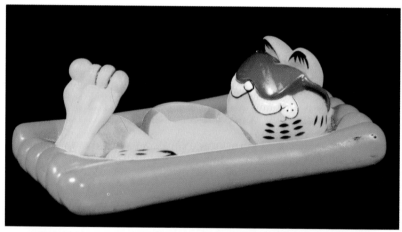

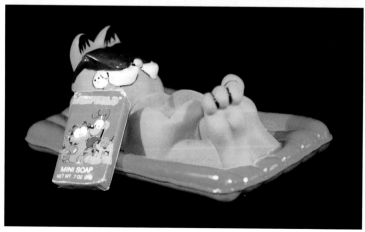

Garfield bandages.
Quantasia. $5-8.

Car floor mat made of rubber. Odie
and Garfield. $15-20.

Rubber Garfield porch mat. Raises lettering and Garfield. $20-25

Other Garfield collectibles available but not shown:

Ceramic mugs:
Garfield in devil suit. "Last of the red hot lovers." $5-10.
Garfield in love. "Love and hearts all over cup." $5-10.
Garfield as a Bill's fan. "I'm a Bills fan-atic." $5-10.
Garfield with Arlene. "I like you because your soft." $5-10.
Garfield as a graduate. "I finally did it." $5-10.
Garfield in sunglasses. "Cool daddy." $5-10.
Garfield writing X's and O's. "Hugs and kisses." $5-10.
Garfield laying down laughing. "I like you cause your funny." $5-10.
Arlene with red kissing lips. "Together." $5-10.

Ceramic Enesco Figurines:
Garfield graduate. "Look out world, here I come." $35-45.
Garfield in cast and crutches. "Klutz." $35-45.
Garfield with apple for teacher. "Look we could all use brownie points." $35-45.
Garfield with picture of himself. "I think I'm in love." $35-45.
Garfield in bunny outfit holding carrot. "Here comes kitty cotton." $35-45.
Garfield with tie. "To Dad, from a chip off the old block." $35-45.
Green Odie laying down with big belly. "Must have been something I ate." $35-45.
Odie with tongue hanging out. "Arf " on base. $35-45.
Odie with trophy. "I love bones." $35-45.
Garfield at desk. "I'm so happy here I could barf." $35-45.
Garfield holding mug in Irish outfit "We're all Irish one day a year." $35-45.
Odie and Garfield as Laurel and Hardy. "This is another fine mess you've gotten us into." $50-60.
Jogging Garfield. $20-30.
Garfield with basketball. $20-30.
Garfield with baseball. $20-30.
Garfield roller skating. $20-30.
Garfield playing tennis. $20-30.
Garfield playing hockey with a smile and a tooth missing. $25-35.
Odie with Easter basket and eggs. $45-55.

Plastic figurines:
Garfield as a teacher. "I need substitute students." $30-40.
Garfield as a Doctor. "One x-ray is worth a thousand dollars." $30-40.
Garfield with Arlene. "Where have you been all my life?" $30-40.

Gum ball machines and banks:

Garfield sitting on top of machine. TimMee Toys. 8", $25-35.

Clear glass, sitting Garfield gum ball bank 7", $15-20.

Plastic standing Garfield with football on top of gum ball machine. Bee International. 9.5", $20-30.

Plastic Garfield standing with basketball. Bee International. 9.5", $20-30.

Plastic gum ball machine with Garfield as a baseball player. Bee International. $20-30.

Plastic gum ball machine with Garfield as a soccer player. Bee International. $20-30.

Fat Garfield with flowers on his orange body and white feet. "Think of all the money you could save for lasagna." Matscot Ind. 8.5", $40-50.

Ceramic Garfield bank. "Donations accepted," on his tee- shirt. Enesco Corp. 6", $75-100.

Ceramic, sitting Garfield holding fork and spoon, bank. "Feed the Kitty," on his bib. Enesco Corp. 6", $75-100.

Collectors plates: Danbury Mint

Garfield on table ready to pounce on dessert. "And now for dessert." 8", $60-75.

Garfield writing a letter. "I met a charming cat in the mirror this morning." 8",
$60-75.

Garfield sleeping in his exercise outfit. "Sleep, the perfect exercise." 8", $60-75.

Telephones:

Plastic Garfield in standing position and holding white phone. Tyco Indus. Says 11 different things. $125-150.

One piece plastic Garfield phone. Pick up Garfield and he opens and closes his eyes. Buttons in belly. Kash N Gold Ltd. Telemania. $75-100.

Plastic Garfield laying down, telephone. Head rotates to each side. Tyco Industries. Push buttons in receiver in back. $75-100.

Miscellaneous Collectibles:

Plastic talking camera. Talks as you shoot the pictures. Says "Come on.. Look like your having fun," and "OK everyone.. no smile, no cake and ice cream," and "party on." 35mm. $30-40.

Plush bean bags. Garfield, Arlene, Pooky, Nermal, Odie. $8-10 each.

Resin sculpture statue of Garfield. Over 9" tall. Caption on base 'Big Fat Hairy Deal.' $30-40.

Vinyl toilet seat. Appliquéd Garfield. "Protected by an attack cat." $15-20.

Plush Garfield door draft protector. "Draft dodger." 36". $15-20.

Vinyl, sitting Garfield bank. 7 1/4". $10-15.

Plush Garfield backpack. Zipper on top of Garfield's head. $15-20.

Insulated 16 oz. mug. Came with color mini poster. $8-12.

Simulated leather Garfield attaché' case. "Classic Gear" logo. Garfield embroidered on front. $50-75.

Garfield down loading rug. 35" x 22". "Help I'm down loading and I can't get up."   Garfield is laying on the floor in his chair. $15-20.

Nylon yarn rug. Garfield eating daisies. 35" x 22". $15-20.

Garfield beach towels. Garfield in life guard chair.

Garfield surfing with Odie hanging on. Terry cloth. 30" x 60". $20-25.

Plastic Garfield hand held massager. $15-20.

Plush, full- figure Garfield stuffed toy. 34" tall. $150-200.

Plastic Garfield solar calculator. 3.5" x 5". $15-20.

Plastic Garfield bag clip. 5". $5-8.

Wind up Garfield music box and figurine. Garfield is in bed eating breakfast with Pooky, by his bedside, and Odie giving him attention. 8.5" x 9.5". $100-150.

Plastic Garfield FM mini portable radio. $20-30.

Garfield fun facts:

01.)Garfield got his name from Jim Davis's grandfather.. Jim Garfield Davis.

02.)Garfield has a girlfriend (who is a fuzzy pink cat with big red lips) named Arlene.

03.)Garfield likes to chase Odie, the dog, around, push him off the table, and harass him. Odie is a lively, spirited, yellow dog with big eyes and a long tongue that is usually hanging out.

04.)Garfield has a teddy bear named Pooky, that he found in a drawer. Garfield likes to hug him.

05.)Jon Arbuckle is the cartoonist in the column who adopted Garfield.

06.)Nermal is the gray cat friend of Garfield's who belongs to Jon's grandfather.

07.)Garfield's birthday is June 19, 1978.

08.)Monday the 13th is his worst day.

09.)Garfield likes his coffee strong enough to sit up and bark.

10.)Garfield loves himself more than anybody else. He thinks he is cute, funny, lovable, and humble.

11.)According to Garfield, when you cross a dog and a cat you get a stupid cat.

12).All food is good.

13.)One of Garfield's favorite sayings is "Big Fat Hairy Deal."

14.)Garfield keeps his affection in the closet.

15.)Garfield says of age that he is old enough to know better and young enough not to care.

16.)Garfield's best time in life is breakfast, lunch and supper.

Want more Garfield fun facts? Visit http:// www.garfield.com.

Also available are the "Garfield Stuff" catalogues. To order one 1-888-274-paws (7297).

Bibliography

Braun, Debra. Garfield Collectibles. Atglen, Pa: Schiffer Pub. Ltd., 1998.

Davis, Jim. The Garfield Trivia Book. New York: Ballantine Books, Div. of Random House Inc. 1986.

Garfield Stuff Catalogues. 1997-1998. 5804 Churchman By-Pass, Indianapolis, Ind.

http://www.garfield.com

Karl, Denise. The Garfield Connection Newsletter. Armonk, New York. 1997.